tap water & tidal waves

All proceeds from the sale of this book support the continued work of Global Care.

www.globalcare.org.uk

Registered charity 1054008

©2010 Fiona Castle and Carolyn Savjani

First published in 2011 by
Global Care Publishing, 2 Dugdale Road, Coventry CV6 1PB

All rights reserved.

No part of this publication may be reproduced or transmitted in any form or by any means, electronic or mechanical, including photocopying, recording or any information storage and retrieval system, without the written permission of the authors.

Layout by The Small Marketing Company

All photographs Global Care or used with permission.
Featured photograph on page 9 ©David Sacks/The Image Bank/Getty Images

All quotations used by permission/permission sought
Back cover quotation: Reproduced with permission of Curtis Brown Group Ltd, London on behalf of the Estate of Sir Winston Churchill. ©Winston S. Churchill

Page 44: Beauty for brokenness words used with permission. Graham Kendrick ©1993
Make Way Music www.grahamkendrick.co.uk

ISBN: 978-0-9533929-1-9

Printed in Great Britain for Global Care Publishing by
Clifford Press Limited, Coventry

I recently read a simple quotation which made me weep:

"A child is someone you carry inside you for nine months, on your back or in your arms for three years, and in your heart till the day you die."

It is so true! I have four children and it doesn't matter how old they are, I still hurt when they hurt, weep when they weep, and rejoice when they rejoice. It will never change.

But I have been a very privileged mother. I have been able to provide my children with a loving home, comfortable surroundings and enough good food to grow up strong and healthy.

Sadly, this is not the case for millions of children around the world. The thought of not being able to provide enough food and clothing for my children does not bear thinking about.

How do mothers feel who are in these desperate circumstances? They are totally helpless to change their situations.

What can I do to help? How could I make a difference for any of these people? I confess that I feel helpless too.

Fortunately for thousands of children around the world, Ron Newby did not take that view. He saw one child with a need in Uganda and decided he could do something about it. From that one child began a project which, in twenty five years, has become a charity helping countless children on four continents – Global Care.

Mother Teresa said: "How do you change the world? One life at a time."

The greatest purpose in life must be to spend it on something that will outlast it. Ron certainly used his life in that way, and children are still benefiting, way beyond his sad death in 2008.

I remember him teaching me to say: "We can't do everything, but we mustn't do nothing."

I have had the privilege, over the last ten years, of visiting many countries where children are supported by Global Care, so the following pages will include anecdotes of these experiences as well as some written by project leaders and other supporters. There will also be comments by the children themselves.

There is a saying that contentment comes, not from the acquisition of all we want, but from gratitude for all we have.

I have been astounded, as I have travelled to many poverty-stricken countries, by the contentment of people who have so very little. It has humbled me and made me ashamed of my complacency, when I have so much.

Since these visits I have asked God to give me a heart of gratitude for all He has provided for me.

As you read this book and pray for so many needy children, thank God too for all the good things He has given you.

Be challenged! Be prayerful! Be compassionate!

Fiona Castle 2010

Thou has given so much to me. Give me one thing more – a grateful heart.

George Herbert

The greatest thing a man can do for his Heavenly Father is to be kind to some of His other children.

Henry Drummond

Thousands of young adults in the developing world today owe their livelihoods – some their very lives – to the tireless work of UK charity Global Care.

With an unflagging commitment to helping the very poorest of the poor, for over 25 years Global Care has supported vulnerable children in desperate need across Africa, South East Asia and South and Central America as well as in some of Europe's most needy communities.

It's all a far cry from Global Care's humble beginnings as a tiny child sponsorship programme operated from the end of a kitchen table.

It was 1983 and Ron Newby – a senior social worker – had just returned from a visit to Uganda, a country reeling in the aftermath of Idi Amin's horrific regime. Shocked at the sights he witnessed, and the conditions in which he found many orphaned children, Ron was determined to do something to help.

When he failed to attract the support of larger agencies, he decided to go it alone. And so Global Care was born.

Today, more than 25 years later, Global Care is still helping Ugandan children out of poverty through education. The charity is also helping street children, slum children, refugee children, child labourers, orphans and abandoned children in 40 programmes in a further 16 countries on 4 continents.

Global Care has also acquired a proud history of effective and efficient relief aid in some of the world's worst humanitarian disasters, ethnic conflicts and war zones over the past three decades: The Ethiopian famine of 1984, earthquakes in Pakistan, Gujurat and Haiti, the Boxing Day Tsunami of 2004, the Rwandan killing fields, ethnic cleansing in Kosovo, Kurds fleeing Saddam's genocide, war in Mozambique, Lebanon and Iraq... the list goes on.

Although Ron died in 2008, his legacy endures: Through the efforts of generous UK donors and an international staff team, Global Care continues to support vulnerable children, impact needy communities and change lives forever.

Carolyn Savjani 2010

Death comes to all, but great achievements build a monument which shall endure until the sun grows cold

Ralph Waldo Emerson

There are 2.2 billion children in the world

1.9 billion live in the developing world

1 billion of these children live in poverty

Almost half the world's children live in poverty

uganda

Do what is right and good in the Lord's sight, so all will go well with you. Deuteronomy 6:18

Widowed Acan Rose cares for her four grandchildren, aged between three and eleven, in a mud hut in rural north Uganda.

Her two sons died of AIDS-related illnesses, and the children's mother abandoned the family to run off with another man.

Rose works hard as a casual labourer – weeding, gardening and fetching water – trying to make ends meet. She grows cassava on land around the hut, and has a precious orange tree.

But it's a real struggle. And in a country where average life expectancy is just 40, Rose, at 55, feels she is living on borrowed time.

Rose has pinned all her hopes on an education for her grandchildren. She knows it is the only way of breaking the poverty cycle for her family, the only way to prevent the decimation of the next generation through ignorance, poverty and disease.

Her oldest grandchild, Betty, has been accepted onto Global Care's sponsorship programme. She receives healthcare, extra feeding and all her educational needs, meaning the family's meagre resources now stretch that little bit further.

Global Care also provided the family with a vaccinated, pregnant goat – a source of milk and income – and a dream come true for Rose.

Rose told me: "The only hope I have for the future is these children. I am getting older, and I am weak, but if they get an education they can care for me. I thank God that since Betty joined the programme she has not been sick. If she had not been taken on I would not manage. It has given her the opportunity to change, she is now a smart girl!

"I thank God for bringing you all the way from England and I pray the Lord God takes you back safely. When you get back tell them you have met Acan Rose and she is so happy, but she still needs support."

Blessed Lord, open our ears to hear what thou speakest and our eyes to see as thou seest. Give us hearts to beat in sympathy with Thine at the sight of every little child; and above all Lord, to understand and experience how surely and how blessedly thou fulfillest thy promise – 'Whoso shall receive one such little child in my name, receiveth me.'

Andrew Murray

Even if my mother and father abandon me, the Lord will hold me close. Psalm 27:10

Tiny baby Ruth miraculously survived being buried alive by her own mother.

As an illegitimate newborn, she was buried alive under a tree in the Ugandan bush – a horrific act of rejection and denial by her distraught mother.

Miraculously, she survived for more than 12 hours because the placenta was still attached, and was discovered the next day by curious children.

Baby Ruth's mother was arrested and imprisoned – but amazingly Ruth was handed back to her. In Uganda, children under five are imprisoned with their parents if there is no-one else to care for them.

Global Care's staff fought to get Ruth freed and arranged for her care while a suitable home could be found.

The little girl now has a home with grandparents, with extra help from Global Care. She is growing and thriving as every little girl should – but her story so nearly had a different ending.

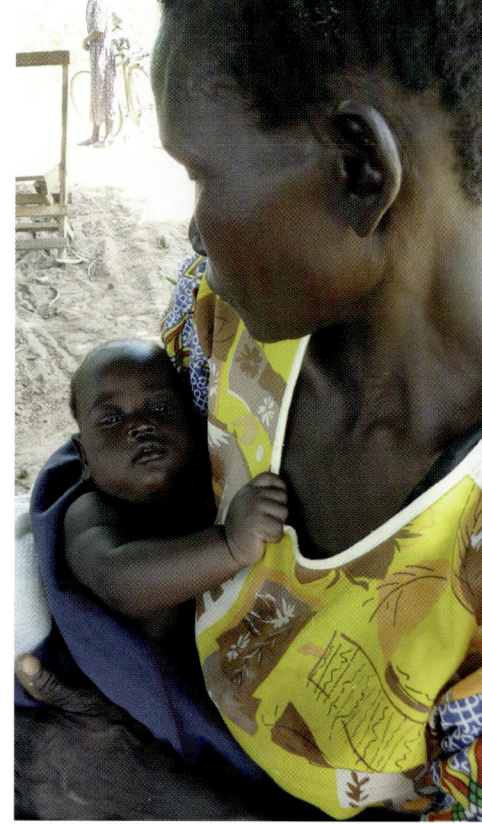

```
Over 9 million children under five die every
year. Most of these deaths occur in two
regions - sub-Saharan Africa and South Asia.
In industrialised countries the figure was
just 100,000.
```

UN 2009

The continuation of this suffering and loss of life contravenes the natural human instinct to help in times of disaster. Imagine the horror of the world if a major earthquake were to occur and people stood by and watched without assisting the survivors!

Yet every day, the equivalent of a major earthquake killing over 30,000 young children occurs to a disturbingly muted response.

They die quietly in some of the poorest villages on earth, far removed from the scrutiny and conscience of the world. Being meek and weak in life makes these dying multitudes even more invisible in death.

UN Progress of Nations report 2000

As a young student, Gertrude Iga won a scholarship to university in Morocco. There she became a Christian – and God prompted her to return to Uganda.

Back in Kampala, she began to teach Sunday school at her local church. She soon realised the children were illiterate, and started teaching them at her home, turning her garage into a classroom. She later employed two teachers to help her. These teachers needed a salary. Gertrude too, needed to earn a living, but the children were from poor families who couldn't contribute to the cost of her teaching.

At this time Gertrude met Ron Newby, founder of Global Care, who offered to sponsor some children so she could continue to teach. After some years Gertrude was able to erect two buildings for the new 'Guiding Star School'. Aware of the problems many pupils were having at home, five years ago Gertrude started a boarding department for these children. Many have since been sponsored by Global Care's supporters, helping them complete their education.

It has been a wonderful experience to visit Guiding Star School on two occasions and witness its ongoing work, often under very difficult circumstances.

Gertrude has a huge heart of compassion for these children, possibly because of her own dysfunctional childhood. Many have been brutalised and beaten by stepmothers and raped by extended family members, desperately vulnerable after their own parents died of AIDS.

One very poignant story was of a couple who had ten children, eight of whom died of AIDS as adults. That left fourteen orphaned grandchildren to look after, five of whom attended Gertrude's school. When two of the children died of AIDS Gertrude visited the elderly grandparents and was able to get sponsorship for all the remaining children. I was able to visit the grandparents, who continue to struggle. Now the grandmother has suffered a stroke, leaving the only remaining adult son to care for them all.

Strength and honour are her clothing. She shall rejoice in time to come. **Proverbs 31:25**

Knowledge is not the most important thing in the world. Love is essential. **Francois Fenelon**

I am walking through the camp, a cluster of ragged children trailing behind.

Two girls wave to me. I stop walking.

Fiona is 18. Rebekah is 19. Teenage mums. Single mums. Rejected by their families, abandoned by the men who made them pregnant. They met, here in the camp, both desperate, both alone. Decided to help each other.

Their babies are tiny and truly beautiful. They invite me in. It is dark and gloomy. Their hut has mud walls, a mud floor and a thatched roof which leaks when it rains. There are a few blankets on the floor, a cooking pot, a few articles of baby clothes. Nothing else.

I can't help remembering what my house looked like when I first became a mum. The Moses basket, pushchair, the cot upstairs, the car seat, the kitchen littered with sterilising equipment... Such a lot of equipment for such a small baby!

Here, there is almost nothing. The contrast is almost too much for me to bear.

What will become of these beautiful little ones?

Fiona and Rebekah shrug and hold the babies closer. They are doing their best. What else can they do?

THANK YOU

... for my electricity bill – my home has light and heat

*Christ has no body now but yours
No hands, no feet, on earth but yours*

*Yours are the eyes through which He looks
With compassion on this world*

*Yours are the feet with which He walks to
do good*

*Yours are the hands
With which He blesses the world*

*Yours are the hands, yours are the feet
Yours are the eyes, you are His body.*

St Therese of Lisieux 1873–97

The mother's heart is the child's classroom. Henry Ward Beecher

bangladesh

God has not given us a spirit of fear and timidity, but of power, love and self-discipline. 2 Timothy 1:7

The land is green and verdant. Fruitful and lush. When the sun shines, it's beautiful.

But extreme weather is a constant risk. Cyclones, hurricanes and flooding occur with devastating regularity.

Poverty is a daily companion for most families, most children, most mothers, in this rural corner of southern Bangladesh.

Three years ago, Purnima Biswas struggled just like everyone else. Pregnant with her second child, she and her four-year-old son relied on her husband's income from casual labour.

But then she joined a group of other mothers in a micro-finance initiative established by Global Care.

It's a simple self-help concept. The mothers agree to save just a few taka each week from their meagre income, paying the money into a central account.

Once they have saved a certain amount, they become eligible to take a loan to help establish an enterprise. Maybe buying chickens so they can sell eggs. Or buying fishing nets so their husbands can work independently.

Purnima saw this as her chance to make a difference, and she saved diligently.

Eventually she was able to take a loan. She opened a market stall selling tea. The business took off. The loan was repaid. She took out another one, expanding the business.

Now it's a bustling tea shop, which she runs with her husband's help. Her little girl is now two and a half, and her son, now seven, is a student at Global Care's pre-school in Horintana.

Life is looking bright for this little family.

A hand up, not a hand out. That's what it's all about.

In His love He clothes us, enfolds and embraces us; that tender love completely surrounds us, never to leave us.

Julian of Norwich

Tapon lives in a small roadside hut made of rice leaves.

He shares the single room with his mother, grandmother, brother and sister.

It barely shelters them – when the rain comes the floor turns to mud and everything gets wet. It's hard to sleep, let alone study, in these conditions.

His mother does her best to scrape a living – she goes fishing or cleans for a well-to-do family. But often it's not enough, and the family goes hungry.

They have just one hope: Tapon attends the pre-school in Horintana funded by Global Care.

Perhaps through education he can build a better future for himself and his family?

Children are the anchors that hold a mother to life. **Sophocles**

1 in 3 children in the developing world do not have adequate shelter

Little Amina was just nine when she fell ill with acute appendicitis. It's an illness which can be cured with a routine operation.

In rural Bangladesh this simple operation costs $100 – just £60 – and that was a sum far beyond the reach of Amina's poverty-stricken parents.

Yet Amina fell ill while Global Care's UK volunteers were visiting her home village. They were able to pay for the operation and bring Amina back to health and strength. They saved her life.

But for thousands of children like Amina, there are no rich Westerners around to save the day.

THANK YOU

... for my electricity bill – my home has light and heat

...that the cash machine is out of order – I have money in the bank to provide for my family

```
Infectious and treatable
diseases other than HIV
continue to blight the
lives of the poor across
the world.
2.2 million children die
because they are not
immunized. One million die
from malaria alone.
1.8 million children die
every year from diarrhoea
```

UN Human Development Report
2006 & 2007

cambodia

The hardest job you'll ever love is being a mother   Anon

One of my heroes is a man called Rostitus Cheng. I met him when I visited Cambodia.

His father was murdered by the Khmer Rouge and his brother died of starvation. Rostitus and his mother fled to Thailand, where he found food on a rubbish dump to survive. But his mother sickened and died, and Rostitus became a street child.

Amazingly, a Christian woman took him in and he became her adopted son. She helped him study and, as he said, "loved him as her own son."

When peace came, he and his adoptive mother came back to Cambodia and, eventually, moved to Poi Pet, on the Thai border.

In recent years Poi Pet has become the Las Vegas of Cambodia. Multi-million dollar buildings stand amongst the abject poverty of the rest of the town, and here Rostitus saw many street children and orphans.

Reminded of his past life – and the love of his adoptive mother – he determined to make a difference by starting a children's home. As his mother had before him, he loved these adopted children as if they were his own.

However, by the time he had 20 children living in the home, it was a struggle to feed and clothe them, and he was grateful to be put in touch with Global Care, who began to support the children through sponsorship.

With Global Care's help he also began a feeding programme for street children in Poi Pet, which developed into an informal school. Leaving the work in Poi Pet in capable hands, he then moved to Cambodia's capital, Phnom Penh, and started a school for children living and working in appalling conditions on a rubbish dump.

Even though the dump has now closed, Rostitus remains committed to supporting these families, who have now lost their only source of income, helping their children achieve a better future through education.

All these amazing initiatives have been borne out of one man's understanding of the plight of others, through his own suffering – and the loving heart of a woman who took a child from the streets as her own.

The joy on the faces of the children in the orphanage was overwhelming. They were so proud of what they were doing! They all had a real and visible faith in the Lord Jesus and *they* even prayed for *me*!

Rostitus has made such a difference to so many children and changed their destiny, by using the gifts God has given him.

Who knows what would have happened to him – and to all these other children – if his lovely adoptive mother had not looked with compassion on that lost little boy?

I think it must somewhere be written that the virtues of mothers shall be visited on their children. Charles Dickens

13-year-old Payne Chan always longed to go to school. But his parents couldn't afford to send him – or any of his seven siblings.

Instead he worked on Phnom Penh's municipal rubbish dump, one of hundreds of children scavenging for items which could be sold.

Until Global Care opened its New Hope Centre on the edge of the dump, offering children a basic education – free of charge!

Payne Chan was one of the first pupils. He carried on working on the dump at weekends, to help supplement the family income.

But every weekday you'll find him at the New Hope Centre, learning to read and write, doing his sums, pursuing his dream.

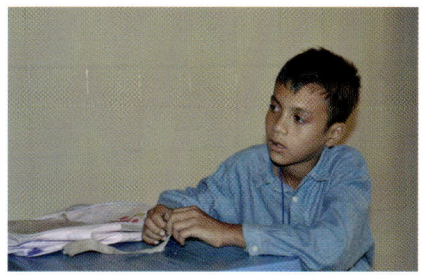

Those who oppress the poor insult their Maker,
but those who help the poor know Him.

Proverbs 14:31

Our lives end, the day we become silent about the things that matter   Martin Luther

Around 45% of Cambodian children aged 5-14 are involved in child labour activities (UNICEF)

Around 180 million children under 18 are currently risking long term damage to their health because of their dangerous work.

Poi Pet literally was a hell hole. There are no words to describe how bad this town was. Just knee deep in rubbish, mud and filth everywhere. We saw whole families on the street, young girls aged 6-9 looking after 3 younger siblings, carrying a baby – it was all very upsetting.

We also saw lines of young adult girls, prostitutes, standing there, and men just walking down the line and choosing one. It wasn't at all hidden. We felt in absolute shock and despair, thinking 'where is the hope in this place?'

Then we walked into the centre and there were these kids, just street kids, and they were having school and just to see them doing school, you thought 'here's the hope, in what Global Care is doing.'

We helped feed them – they just sat in their rows and waited until you put the food down, waited their turn. Some of them ate it all in one go, others were putting it in bags, some wolfed it down, some asked for more.

It was just an incredible and humbling experience. We left there thinking 'there's quite a bit of hope here.'

Samantha, UK volunteer

When I also visited these street children to witness the feeding programme, I was warned not to wear anything of value as they were skilled in pickpocketing! In the event I found the children to be polite, well mannered and so grateful. That day we were able to provide them with a gift of extra fruit. Many children chose not to eat that fruit, but to take it back to share with other family members – a humbling experience!

It is when God seems to have abandoned us that we must abandon ourselves most wholly to God

Francois Fenelon

THANK YOU

... for my electricity bill – my home has light and heat

...that the cash machine is out of order – I have money in the bank to provide for my family

... for feeling ill – I know I can visit a doctor

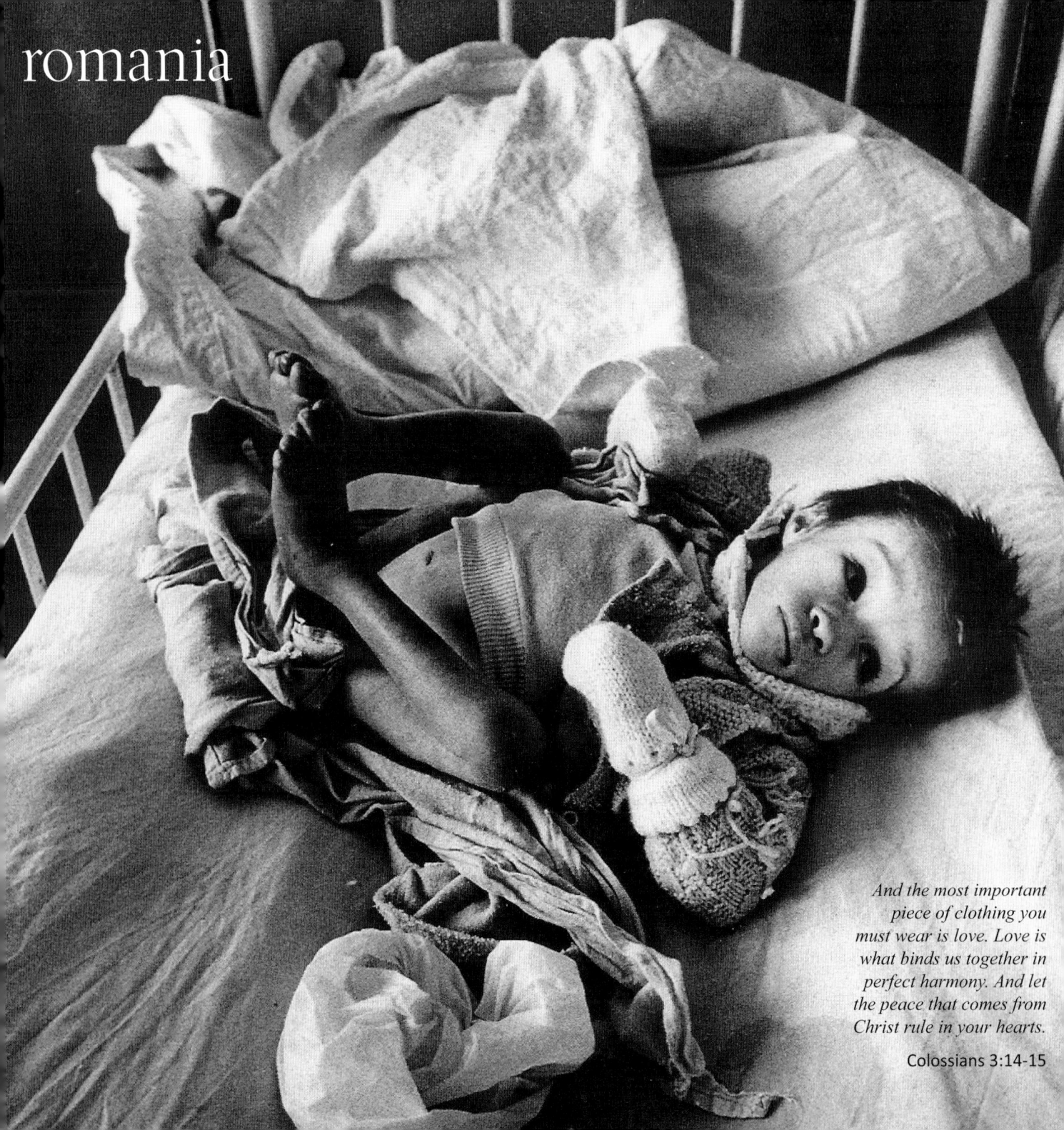

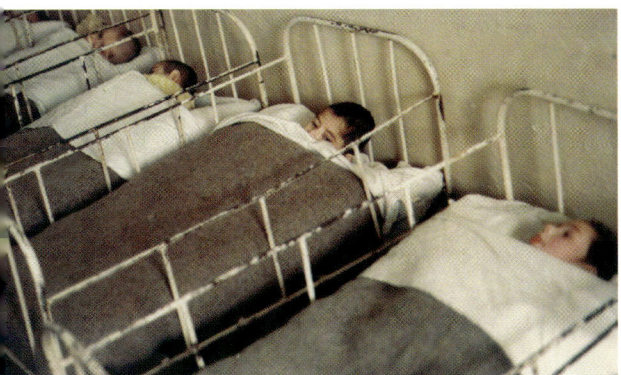

Thousands of unwanted children confined in urine-soaked cots, emaciated, vacant-eyed... No-one will ever forget the horrific pictures which emerged when Romania's Communist dictatorship fell and the country's orphanages opened to the watching West.

Global Care was one of the first charities to win permission to take care of children from the infamous orphanages. Casa Sperantei (Home of Hope) was acquired in April 1992, and by the end of August, had become home to 12 children. The oldest was 7 ½, the youngest, just 4.

The Romanian authorities classed all our children as mentally retarded, due to the total lack of stimulation received. They believed none would ever succeed in education or hold down a job. They were wrong.

Almost 20 years later, all have completed High School and a number have graduated from university. All are either still in education or working independently.

Truly the Home of Hope was well-named.

It was hard when I came here the first time, it was very hard. The children were all so sad, so very sad. But they worked hard with the mammas, and all the mammas took the children to their hearts. To me they were like they were my children – I have five children and four grandchildren but many more children at Casa Sperantei. And I had a special place for the two babies – Reka and Johnny. It has been a privilege to be here, to be a mamma to these children.

Mamma Rodica, The Home of Hope, Global Care Romania

And look at those children! They sit around your table as vigorous and healthy as young olive trees.

Psalms 127:3

Ioanut was six when he came to the Home of Hope. He has since completed High School and studied art. Ioanut is now 24, living and working independently, with his own home, and a full-time job in retail.

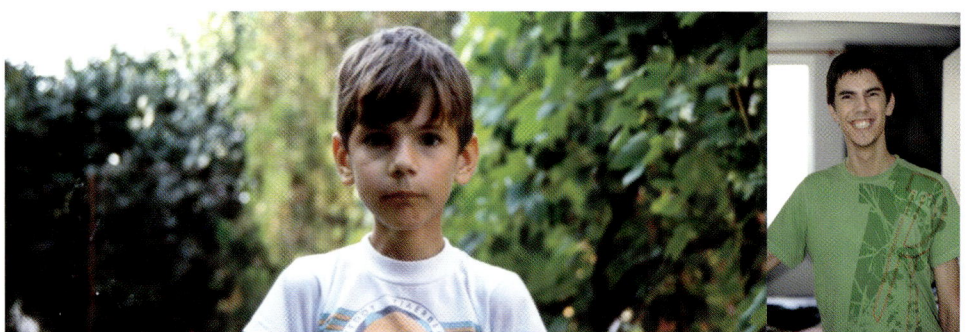

Before, in the orphanage, we shared many kids to one room, sometimes it was cold. We were not really naked but not many clothes. We didn't go to school or any special activities, we just played outside with nobody.

When I first came here, the mammas were here, and we had many toys and TV for the first time. There were just three boys together in my room and it was nice.

If I just lived there (the state orphanage) for 18 years then maybe I wouldn't be where I am now. Global Care brought me out of there and they brought me here, and that's something special.

Ioanut, Romania

Before we came here we were living in a big house with very many children, with hundreds of children, but we didn't know each others names. They had many children from different backgrounds – Hungarian, Roma – but we didn't know anyone. Here (at the Home of Hope) we were friends, good friends. We are still friends, we are like a family.

Vera, now 24, is studying nursing part-time and will qualify soon. She is also working long hours as a chambermaid in a hotel. Vera has huge determination to succeed.

My mother she just left me with the mammas, and she told the mammas if they didn't take me she would leave me here. I think she stayed with me six weeks and then she left me and I don't know who she is and I didn't see her never.

'At least she picked a good place?' I suggest. Reka shrugs. An insensitive question.

There is never a good place to be abandoned.

Reka, Romania

Probably I wouldn't be alive if I hadn't come to the Home of Hope. I needed three heart operations, and the fact that I was put in an orphanage shows me that my natural birth parents couldn't afford my surgery. If they couldn't afford the first, then they couldn't have afforded the second or third. So I don't know what would have happened to me.

Mihai, Romania

The person who has stopped being thankful has fallen asleep in life. RL Stevenson

THANK YOU

... for my electricity bill – my home has light and heat

...that the cash machine is out of order – I have money in the bank to provide for my family

... for feeling ill – I know I can visit a doctor

... for missing my train – because public transport is readily available

colombia and honduras

Enedes works as a house mother at Futuro Juvenil, a home for former street children in Colombia, supported by Global Care

"I was going through a hard time here – a small group of children were behaving badly and one boy threw something at my leg which left me with bruises. I was trying to adapt to being here but it was hard so I thought that this was not the place God wanted me to be.

"I prayed and asked God if it was right to leave the home. I packed my bags and was planning to leave the next day, but before I went to bed I checked on all the children and kissed them goodnight.

"In one room all the boys were asleep apart from one of the most rebellious boys, Carlos – the one who had hurt my leg. He sat up in bed and said he just wanted to tell me something. At this stage I hadn't told the children I was going to leave the next morning.

"Carlos then said he just wanted to give me a hug and say that he loved me very much. I received his hug and his love and felt that God was saying I was to stay on in the home, so I went back to my room and unpacked all my things and I am still here today."

Children have more need of models than critics

Joseph Joubert

And we know that God causes everything to work together for the good of those who love God and are called according to His purpose for them

Romans 8:28

Little Ever Ezequiel ended up on the streets when his dad died. His mum had abandoned them both years before, and so Ever, at just eight years old, was left to fend for himself.

Ever survived alone until July 2008, when Global Care's Honduran partners arranged for him to join their home for former street children; Project Manuelito.

But although he settled in at the home, enjoying the company, the warmth, the food, his heart was restless.

Surely his mother was out there somewhere? Surely she'd take him back? Surely she wouldn't abandon him again?

In April 2009 he ran away. Our anxious staff searched the streets for him, to no avail.

"It was hard for us, our family at Manuelito, because each of them has a special place in our hearts," recalls director Jorge Pinto. "We looked for him with no success at all, time went by and our hope of finding him was gone."

But in December 2009 Jorge received a phone call – Ever had been found! Jorge walked out of his meeting and drove for miles to the city of Juticalpa.

He writes: "When I went into the office I was surprised from behind by some hands that were hugging me, it was Ever Ezequiel. He was wearing some tight jeans that didn't fit him, barefooted, with a purple eye, swollen face and some skin problems.

"When I began to talk to him, he manifested with tears that he couldn't find his mother and that maybe she was dead by now.

"The truth is, Ever, that missing kid of Manuelito, is back not only with health problems but also problems in his soul that only God can heal.

"Yesterday he slept in my house, I bathed him, my wife and I cared for him, and really early in the morning – 4.45am – I went to see him in his room where he was deeply asleep, where he can elude all his pain and dream of a better morning.

"While I am writing all these thoughts I can't stop crying and telling the Lord – thank you for this Christmas gift!"

The Eternal God is your refuge and His everlasting arms are under you.   Deuteronomy 33: 27

When there's love at home there's beauty all around.   Anon

I was living in the streets from the age of three. My dad left my mum when she was pregnant with me.

The streets were my home and we made a place to live out of cardboard and it was really difficult for us as it kept falling down and so we had to just sleep on the ground, covering ourselves with plastic.

Sometimes we would eat and sometimes we would go without. Once I had to steal so I could buy some food for my mum.

It was very complicated for us living like this, not knowing if we were going to be alive or dead, or what would happen to us the next day, or if we would be able to find food to eat.

When I was ten I got to know pastor Pinto and he asked me to swap my glue for food.

We went to visit, but we would hide our drugs in the bushes so he didn't take them from us. We would eat, watch films, talk, and then go back to the streets. This was the hardest bit, so we would sit outside the restaurants and beg for food.

I remember when they started to build the home. I went to see it and told my mum I wanted to live in the Manuelito home and she said 'yes'.

This made me happy because I never imagined having a home to live in, for me it was very impressive. I didn't know that God had many plans for my life and now my life has changed so much. I am very happy as Manuelito is not just a project it is a home.

Maricela is studying hard and hopes to go to university soon.

I am so very grateful to God for giving me this opportunity to realise the dreams I had in my heart even though I didn't know I had dreams in my heart. I now have a future. I know I can see my family and that I can soon work so I can help them and encourage them forwards. I am very happy here and thankful to God for having a home.

Without dreams you may continue to exist, but you have ceased to live.   Mark Twain

I waited patiently for the Lord to help me, and he turned to me and heard my cry. He lifted me out of the pit of despair, out of the mud and the mire. He set my feet on solid ground and steadied me as I walked along. He has given me a new song to sing, a hymn of praise to our King. Many will see what He has done and be astounded. They will put their trust in the Lord.

Psalm 40:1-3

THANK YOU

... for my electricity bill – my home has light and heat

...that the cash machine is out of order – I have money in the bank to provide for my family

... for feeling ill – I know I can visit a doctor

... for missing my train – because public transport is readily available

... when my washing machine breaks down – I wash my children's clothes with little effort

```
An estimated 40
million children
live and work on
the streets of
Latin America
```

Blessed are those who are generous because they feed the poor.

Proverbs 22:9

ethiopia, morocco and dr congo

Nine-year-old Hiajmant lives with her widowed mother and four siblings.

Her father died four years ago, after falling ill with a 'sickness' – believed to be AIDS related.

It's up to her mum to support the family. And she is doing her best.

Uneducated and unskilled, living in a small township with limited industry, her only option is to take on any casual job she can find – fetching water, cleaning houses… It's back-breaking and soul-destroying, but it's all there is.

And with five young mouths to feed, she has to keep going.

Her great hope is that, one day, things will be different.

Thanks to Global Care, Hiajmant is now in school. And she's not just in school – she's top of her class!

Hiajmant joined our pre-school in Jajura, Ethiopia, 18 months ago. When September comes, she will join a government school – with every chance of success.

Prior to the opening of Global Care's pre-schools, children from peasant families like Hiajmant's very rarely attended school and even when they did, drop-out rates were high.

But two years of non-formal education is giving these children a fantastic foundation on which to build – an academic headstart and a bucketload of confidence.

And most of all it is giving them hope. Hope of more than just grinding poverty, hunger and back-breaking labour. Hope of a future that is brighter than their parents' wildest dreams.

Nine-year-old Hanan used to be top of her class. But this bright little girl hasn't been to school for a year.

Her family keep her at home in Morocco, helping with the chores, because they just can't afford to send her.

Just catching the bus to the nearest school, four miles away, costs more than her father earns. There's no money at all for a uniform, or school materials…

Everything changed for the better when Hanan was accepted onto Global Care's sponsorship scheme.

Now the little girl is living with her aunt in the city where she can walk to school. Sponsorship pays for her uniform, her school equipment and her health and welfare needs.

Hanan's future looks a lot brighter now.

You need not cry very loud – He is nearer to us than we think

Brother Lawrence

In Africa, children of mothers who have completed five years of primary education are 40% more likely to live beyond the age of five

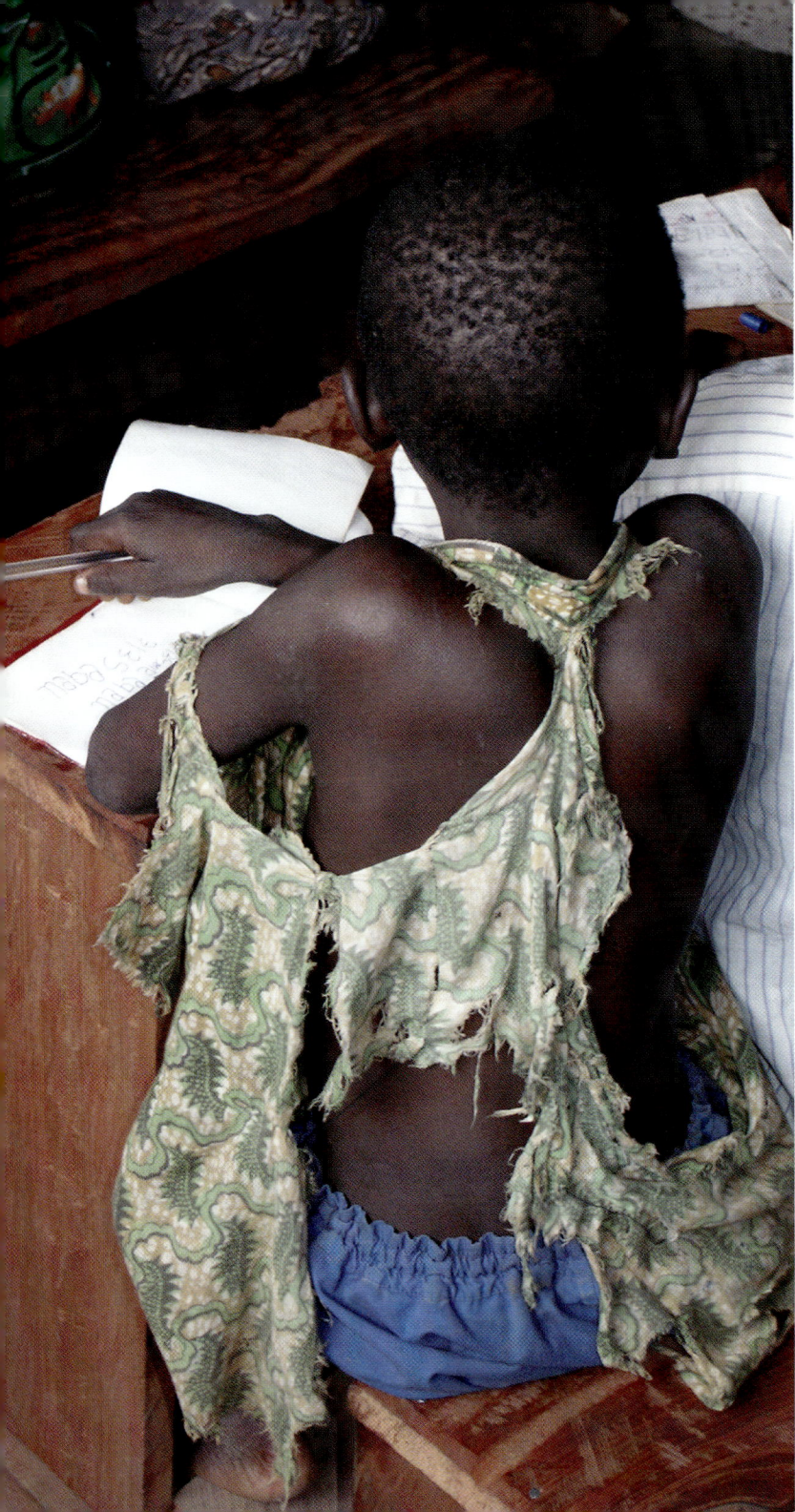

Over 115 million children, the majority of them girls, are still denied the right to go to school.

An educated girl marries later and has fewer children. Her children are more likely to survive, be healthy and go to school. She will be more productive at home and better paid in the workplace. She will be better able to protect herself against HIV, trafficking and abuse. Girls' education breaks the poverty cycle!

I will pour out my Spirit and my blessings on your children.

Isaiah 44:3

This heart-warming story is from a headteacher at a school in a Global Care-supported literacy programme in Ngbaka, DR Congo:

Deasali's family were having trouble breeding animals – their chickens and goats would die. Advice from the witchdoctor didn't help.

One day Deasali came home with a school book and read aloud to all the family about looking after chickens; keeping them in an enclosure, giving them clean water and other ideas. Her father was impressed that she could read their language, and agreed to try out some of the ideas.

The headteacher writes: "I met her father the other day. He said that this year for the first time their chickens and goats were healthy, and they had already made some money from them. He told me: 'I was worried at the idea of a girl going to school, because I was afraid it would turn her into a loose living woman. But now I see the point of being able to read books. The children learn things that help improve our lives! Now I'm going to send some of my other children to school'."

THANK YOU

... for my electricity bill – my home has light and heat

...that the cash machine is out of order – I have money in the bank to provide for my family

... for feeling ill – I know I can visit a doctor

... for missing my train – because public transport is readily available

... when my washing machine breaks down – I wash my children's clothes with little effort

... when the kids are late home from school – education is free for every child in the UK

The consciousness of children is formed by the influences that surround them; their notions of good and evil are the result of the moral atmosphere they breathe.

Jean Paul Richter

sponsorship

All the flowers of all the tomorrows are in the seeds of today.

Chinese Proverb.

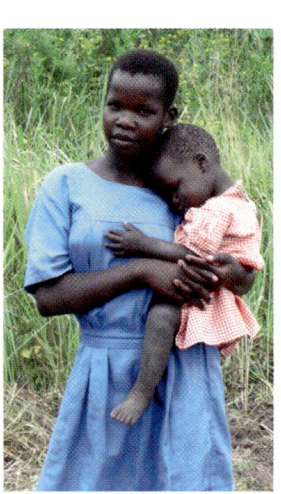

On a trip to Uganda, I made a "home visit" to a family, deep in the bush, because the oldest child, who was sponsored, had not been attending school.

We discovered ten-year-old Dhembe struggling to look after her six siblings, including two month old twins, because her mother had gone mad and run away.

It became apparent that after each birth she had suffered from post natal depression, but no diagnosis or treatment was available.

The father was a peasant labourer, with no education, who scratched a living as a woodcutter, earning barely enough to provide a bottle of milk a day.

The difficulties that so many of these people suffer make our own problems pale into insignificance. Visiting such families changes one's outlook for ever.

Global Care has now supplied the family with gardening tools and a vaccinated, pregnant goat. Dhembe has now been able to resume her education, which is the only gift which can provide a better tomorrow.

Be Still

Be still my child and do not fear

Be still my child for I am here

Know peace precious child for a broken past

Know peace precious child free from pain at last

Rise up my child for I adore you

Rise up my child I gave my life for you

Find strength my daughter in my name

Find strength my daughter feel no shame

My beautiful daughter know your worth

My beautiful daughter through my eyes look first

Naomi Hill
October 2009

Way back in 1991, after being abandoned by my father, dumped in a camp with my mother, feeding on other people's leftovers, washing and fetching water for people for food, by God's grace Global Care picked me and brought me to this level – completing secondary education and training as a teacher.

It was a big change in my life situation, a big change for my family, a big change for my community. Surely many in my clan cannot believe how I have climbed the ladder to this level. My family, myself and my community are very proud of Global Care.

I just want to take this opportunity to say thank you to all the supporters, those whom the Spirit of the Lord has touched to sacrifice their efforts, resources and time together for the purpose of supporting me. What a wonderful support. God bless you. I surely have no words to explain or express the joy and happiness I have.

Oumo David, former sponsored child

The consciousness of loving and being loved brings a warmth and richness of life that nothing else can bring.

Oscar Wilde

The unfailing love of the Lord never ends! By his mercy we have been kept from complete destruction. Great is His faithfulness; His mercies begin afresh each day. Lamentations 3: 22-23

On a trip to Uganda I met a gorgeous little girl called Teddy! Because she was so adorable, she had earned the nickname Ah Teddy!

I had the opportunity to play and sing songs with her and then she took me to meet her older sister, Joy. How different this little girl was. Her face was sad, her complexion sallow and she had no energy for games. I overheard some leaders saying that she had full-blown AIDS and that unless she could get a sponsor immediately, in order to receive medication, she would not survive.

Through Global Care's quick action, a sponsor was found and I saw Joy two years later – a happy, smiling girl who had grown beyond recognition and who was able to attend school!

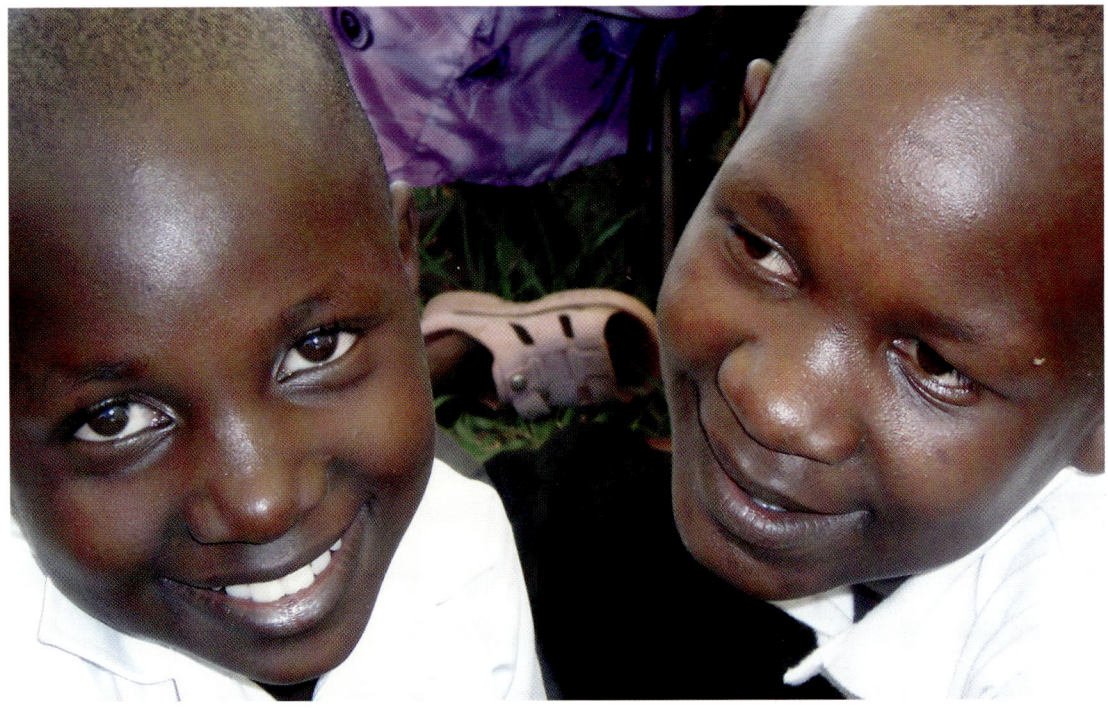

As long as everyone has the means of doing good to his neighbours and does not do so, he shall be reckoned a stranger to the love of God.

Irenaeus

THANK YOU

... for my electricity bill – my home has light and heat

...that the cash machine is out of order – I have money in the bank to provide for my family

... for feeling ill – I know I can visit a doctor

... for missing my train – because public transport is readily available

... when my washing machine breaks down – I wash my children's clothes with little effort

... when the kids are late home from school – education is free for every child in the UK

... when my tummy rumbles – I always provide good food for my children

Nimrod wrote this letter to his sponsor in 2007, just after taking his final exams as a psychology student at Makerere University.

I write this after quite a time of reflection on what it has been like, through the early days of school and how events have unfolded, and realise how thankful and grateful I should really be to you.

The Lord has used you to transform my life. Thank you for loving and accepting me, you took on the responsibility for my education and consequent welfare; that inspired a sense of hope in my life and encouraged me to work even harder… My late daddy passed away when I was only ten, a little boy in primary five; a time when I almost lost hope in life and became desperate but thank God, people of golden hearts such as you still exist in this world I am used to call wicked.

All I wanted to say is that I just cannot seem to thank you enough, but all I can do now is to praise the Lord for you and to pray that he blesses you through this life.

When I met Nimrod in 2009, he was employed in a clinical research centre working with HIV/AIDS victims. He is supporting his sick mother and siblings, and sponsoring his brother until he also graduates from university. He is also developing a poultry unit for 1,000 birds, to increase the family's income.

What can we say about such wonderful things as these? If God is for us, who can be against us? Romans 8:31

When Mother Teresa received her Nobel Prize she was asked 'What can we do to promote world peace?' She replied: "Go home and love your family."

sri lanka

I have come to realise that being unwanted is the worst disease that any human being can experience. Nowadays we have found the medicine for leprosy and lepers can be cured. There's medication for TB and consumption can be cured. But for being unwanted, except there are willing hands to serve and a loving heart to love, I don't think this terrible disease can be cured.

Mother Teresa

Do all the good you can
By all the means you can
In all the ways you can
In all the places you can
To all the people you can
As long as you ever can

John Wesley

A wonderful couple, Tom and Sriyani Tidball tell of some of the work they are doing in partnership with Global Care

One of the earliest groups we helped were 33 Malayalam families we called the Gypsies. Most of the women sold joss sticks, and some read palms and told fortunes, They were the most marginalised of the poor in the area where we ministered. They were isolated and suffered from racial prejudice and extreme poverty. They had originally come as Gypsies from India and spoke their own language of Telagu, as well as Sinhalese and Tamil.

Global Care has been very involved with these 33 families as most of the children came to the Morning Star School funded by Global Care. Most did not have proper documentation, so they stayed at Morning Star, unable to move to a government school. Over the years many of them received an education, learned a vocation and had better opportunities because of Morning Star School.

Before the Tsunami, these families lived on the beach, really close to the shoreline. We knew they were oppressed and we had started looking at ways to get them out of this environment. Most of the men and some of the women were alcoholics, and teenage weddings were a common practice.

Plans were underway to relocate them but then the Tsunami hit our beach, and all 33 homes and their meagre belongings went into the ocean that awful day. Fortunately no one died.

After the Tsunami, they were the first group of people to be provided with homes. CCS and Global Care built them 33 beautiful homes in Dankotuwa. But two weeks before moving in, the host community had an uproar, insisting that these Malayalam people were not welcome, and if they did come, they would be murdered.

CCS went to extreme lengths to fight this, but eventually could not let the families move as their lives were at risk. Other Sinhalese Tsunami families from the CCS community moved to Dankotuwa and the Gypsies stayed in the refugee camp for another two years.

Eventually the government helped them buy land, in Kolannawa. But in the monsoon season it was more like a water hole. Once again CCS raised funds and within a year, with the help of Habitat Sri Lanka, built them homes on very high foundations. Finally, in 2009, they were able to move in.

They have new homes, but still remain marginalised and secluded. Their children still receive help from Global Care, and are trying to make a go of their lives.

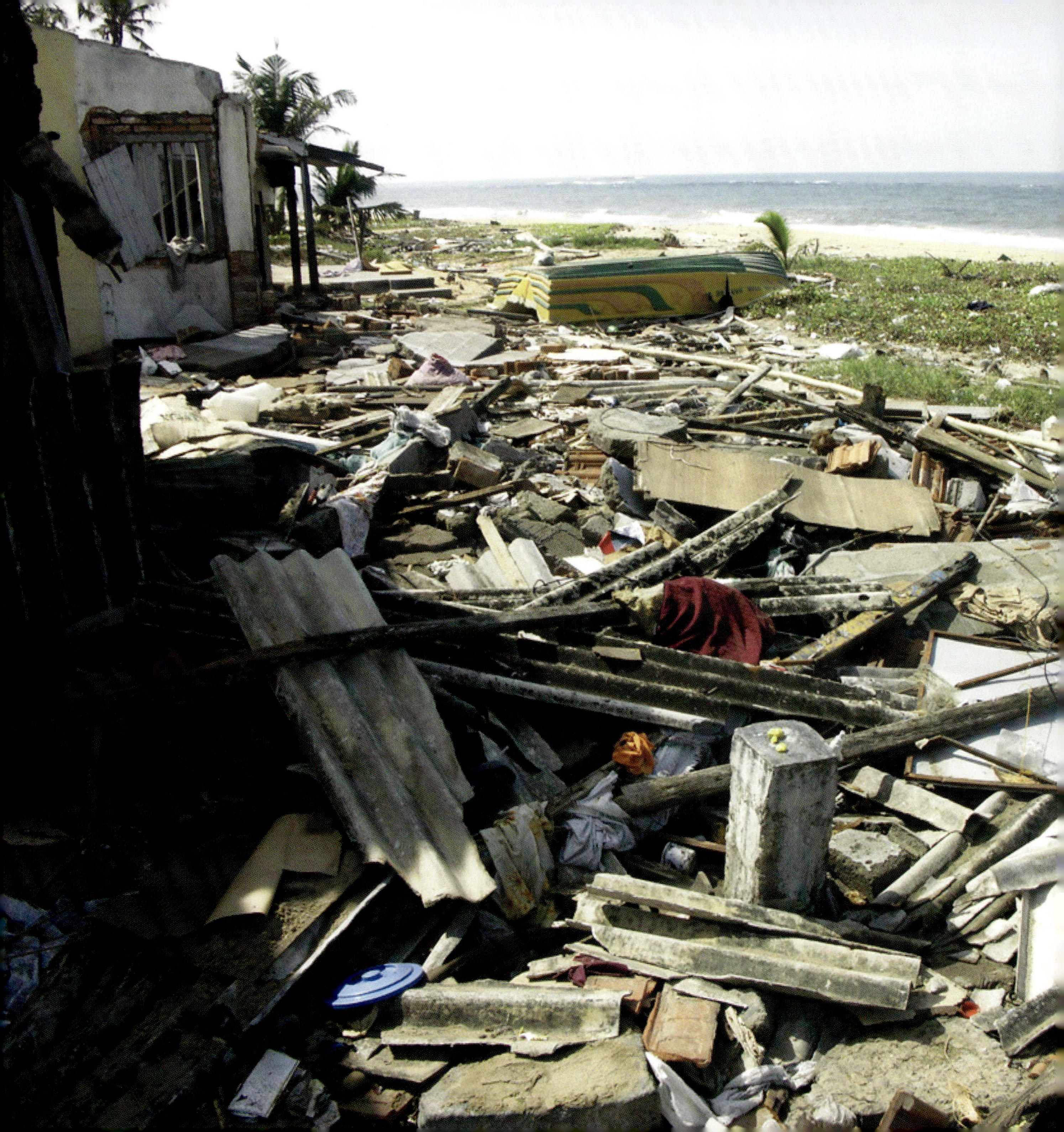

I have visited Sri Lanka twice. The first time was before the Tsunami, when I saw a beautiful beach covered in the worst slum dwellings you could imagine.

This beach was home for 1541 families. However a school, just a few yards from the beach, was available for all the local children.

Supported by Global Care and run by the Community Concern Society (CCS), Morning Star School provided basic education each morning, and a healthy breakfast and lunch.

In the afternoon, vocational training was provided for the older children, giving them hope of a career in the future.

The school also ran a mum and baby clinic, as well as vaccinations and health care for the children.

When the tsunami hit, miraculously no lives were lost – but every one of the slum dwellings was destroyed, leaving families homeless and hopeless.

CCS immediately sprang into action, taking basic food, medical supplies, blankets and water to thousands in the worst hit areas of Sri Lanka, working 24/7.

I knew that 100% of the money Global Care sent out would be used immediately for this relief effort. I was invited to speak about this on Premier Radio, and as a result several churches supported Global Care, trusting that the money would "hit the spot".

I visited Sri Lanka a year later and witnessed the building of many apartments for the fishermen and their families, and other individual family dwellings for so many of the homeless.

In fact one third of all the new housing in the area, post-tsunami, was provided by CCS and their partners, including Global Care. That's a staggering figure – it wasn't just talk, it was ACTION!

An ounce of action is worth a ton of theory
Ralph Waldo Emerson

Mum of three Priyani Soiza had lived on Dehiwela beach for fifty years prior to the Tsunami of Boxing Day 2004.

Her husband, Vijeratan De Silva, worked as a painter, and she took in sewing. Their daughter Ayesha, aged 13, received support with her education through Global Care. Their two older sons worked. The family lived in a simple shack on the beach. Although they were poor, life was stable.

When the tsunami struck Priyani and Vijeratan were at home alone. Priyani was sitting on the doorstep, and, hearing the sound of the sea, seeing boats being tossed up the beach, realised something was wrong. The couple grabbed their most precious electrical possessions – a TV and a fan – and ran, seeing a massive wave coming in as they fled.

They went to an aunt's house, where a message reached them to say their house had been washed away. Priyani recalls: "I burst into tears, I thought things would be water damaged but never thought they would be lost. I thought I would never have anything to replace all those things, it was really hard." They went back the next morning and managed to salvage a single piece of furniture, which they found washed up on the beach.

The family ended up living in the aunt's home for a year, along with three other families – 28 people – most of them living in one room.

Vijeratan suffered from depression after the disaster, so found it difficult to work. He also lost all his business records.

After a year, it became unbearable and they moved back into an empty house near the beach. "We lived in fear of our lives," says Priyani. "We kept a package of documents above the door where it could be grabbed in an emergency. At night if I hear the sea making a noise I can't sleep, I still stir at the slightest noise."

But for Priyani and Vijeratan and their children, the story has a happy ending. In 2007, the family were able to move into a brand new two-bedroom apartment built by Global Care's partners. Their new home is of a far better quality than the shack which was washed away on the beach.

"We sincerely thank you many times for this house," said Priyani. "We do not have the words, we are so thankful for everything."

God is in the slums, in the cardboard boxes where the poor play house. God is in the silence of a mother who has infected her child with a virus that will end both their lives. God is in the cries heard under the rubble of war. God is in the debris of wasted opportunity and lives, and God is with us if we are with them.

Bono

As long as we fail to do anything positive to alleviate suffering, we are merely continuing to contribute to it.

Steve Chalke

THANK YOU

... for my electricity bill – my home has light and heat

...that the cash machine is out of order – I have money in the bank to provide for my family

... for feeling ill – I know I can visit a doctor

... for missing my train – because public transport is readily available

... when my washing machine breaks down – I wash my children's clothes with little effort

... when the kids are late home from school – education is free for every child in the UK

... when my tummy rumbles – I always provide good food for my children

... when my car breaks down – I am privileged to own a car

Those who wait on the Lord will find new strength.

Isaiah 40:31

karenni refugees and thailand

Beauty for Brokenness.
God of the Poor

Beauty for brokenness,
hope for despair,

Lord in your suffering world
this is our prayer

Bread for the children,
justice, joy, peace

Sunrise to sunset,
your Kingdom increase!

Shelter for fragile lives,
cures for their ills

Work for the craftsmen,
trade for their skills

Land for the dispossessed,
rights for the weak

Voices to plead the cause
of those who can't speak.

God of the poor,
friend of the weak

Give us compassion we pray

Melt our cold hearts,
let tears fall like rain

Come, change our love
from a spark to a flame

Graham Kendrick

Most people are aware that Burma is ruled by a brutal military junta, unelected but in power for nearly 50 years.

However few people are aware of the consequences for ethnic minorities within Burma, and fewer still are aware of the plight of the Karenni, inhabitants of the smallest and poorest of the minority states in Burma.

The junta – committed to ethnic cleansing – force the Karenni into relocation camps inside Burma. Rape, forced labour, murder and torture are common.

To escape, the Karenni have two options – to flee to the jungles or to seek asylum in refugee camps along the Thai/Burma border.

Thousands of displaced Karenni are on the run in the jungles – living hand-to-mouth, desperately trying to stay one step ahead of the military forces.

Up to 150,000 more live in closed refugee camps just inside Thailand. They have no right of movement within Thailand and are not allowed to work. Education and training are extremely limited.

Victims of decades of oppression, persecuted, isolated and forgotten by the international community, it would be easy for the Karenni to give up hope.

Global Care is one of a handful of NGOs supporting the Karenni through education, extra feeding and medical and welfare care for children, many of whom are orphaned or separated from parents, living in the camps alone.

My first visit to a Karenni refugee camp took place just before Christmas. The children in the orphanage had rehearsed a nativity play (in English) and they gave me a performance. Given the poverty of their circumstances, their costumes were delightfully imaginative! Afterwards I was asked if I would like them to recite some Bible verses for me. Of course I agreed, and listened for about half an hour while they recited (in English!) Bible verses, one after another! It was humbling. These young children could remember and recite more verses than I ever could. The lovely woman who cared for them told me. "We have nothing, but all the children live and are taught by Bible principles, so that, if ever they are freed, they will have standards to live and work by."

I have visited this area twice and each time I have left my heart behind with these beautiful people. You see, I can't help thinking each night as I climb into my warm bed, knowing I have electricity and plenty of food, that they're still there... still in dire circumstances!

Single mum Anna lives in Thailand. Her seven-year-old son, Paper, is the light of her life.

Anna works for an organization which hands out condoms to the girls who work in the bars around Pattaya – a coastal resort with the reputation as the 'largest brothel in the world'.

But she is also in debt to a loan shark, and in order to stay off the streets herself, she has to work every hour God sends.

Often in the evenings Paper is left home alone, while Anna is out working. But the neighbours keep an eye on him, and she believes he is safe enough…

Until she finds out that a girl has been giving her little boy drugs and cigarettes and encouraging him to watch pornography…

At her wits end, Anna came to the Mercy Centre, a home for children from Pattaya's slums supported by Global Care.

Now Paper is truly safe. He lives at the home, and Anna can see him whenever she wants. He is doing well at school and enjoys art.

Anna is working harder than ever –determined to pay off her debts and build a better future for herself and her son.

We are pressed on every side by troubles, but we are not crushed and broken. We are perplexed, but we don't give up and quit. We are hunted down but God never abandons us. We get knocked down but we get up again and keep going. Through suffering, these bodies of ours constantly share in the death of Jesus, so that the life of Jesus may also be seen in our bodies.

2 Corinthians 5:8-10

Martha is a young mum with two little boys. She lived with her mother, but it was no place of safety.

Her mum would drink heavily and beat Martha and her grandchildren severely. Once she kicked the baby against the wall. Sometimes the mother's boyfriend took her two-year-old son out to meet foreigners… and came back with money for more alcohol.

Martha ran away. She stayed with neighbours, but in the slums of Pattaya, in Thailand, her neighbours were just as poor as she – they couldn't afford to house and feed another family for more than a few days at a time. Sometimes the three of them slept under a tree.

Then a neighbour heard of the Mercy Centre, operated by Global Care's partners. They brought her there for help.

Staff helped Martha find a room of her own, helped with the first month's rent, and provided food and clothes for the children.

They took Martha to the police station and helped her report her mother and her boyfriend for abusing the children.

They helped Martha find a place on a hairdressing course and offered to care for the children while Martha learns skills which will help the whole family stand alone.

Life won't be easy for Martha and the children, who need help to recover from their traumatic past. But now at least they have hope for the future.

THANK YOU

… for my electricity bill – my home has light and heat

…that the cash machine is out of order – I have money in the bank to provide for my family

… for feeling ill – I know I can visit a doctor

… for missing my train – because public transport is readily available

… when my washing machine breaks down – I wash my children's clothes with little effort

… when the kids are late home from school – education is free for every child in the UK

… when my tummy rumbles – I always provide good food for my children

… when my car breaks down – I am privileged to own a car

… when I've lost my specs – I am privileged to be able to see and have been taught to read and write

india

Two of the most inspirational people I have ever known were Vijayan and Premila Pavamani. I met them some years ago.

The streets of Calcutta shocked me. Lined by people living on the pavements, perhaps with tarpaulin to cover them, there was nothing to make life comfortable, which we accept as the 'norm'.

It occurred to me that however hard Global Care worked it would be impossible to eliminate the poverty in this area alone. But Vijayan and Premila were tireless in their efforts to alleviate this despair in as many creative ways as possible.

Vijayan saw beyond their grubby faces and tattered clothes. He dreamed of giving them a chance in life.

In 1978, with a handful of children from one of the worst slums in Calcutta, Vijayan Pavamani started a little school. He invited children to an hour of songs and stories each day.

Gradually, more formal lessons began, and today over 300 children attend Emmanuel School. Admission is reserved for the poorest and there is no fee. The children are mostly slum dwellers – their parents work as vendors, rickshaw pullers and maids. The curriculum ensures academic excellence, enabling the pupils to discover their full potential.

```
Through child sponsorship, Global Care
supports 93 pupils at Emmanuel School.
```

Others might rest on their laurels, but not Vijayan!

Early one morning a group of young beggars stopped him. He took these bedraggled urchins to a nearby tea shop, where they were delighted to be bought food! Vijayan agreed to meet them again, and as contact continued, he discovered they wanted to go to school.

Gradually a small non-formal class developed on the pavement where the children lived. And so the 'Pavement Club' was born.

Today the Pavement Club meets in three locations, including a specially adapted centre, where street children can come for lessons and school children can come for further academic support.

```
Global Care became the main partner supporting the Pavement Club in
1997. Then there were just 30 children. Today over 350 boys and girls
take part.
```

Do not follow where the path may lead. Go instead where there is no path and leave a trail
Ralph Waldo Emerson

Leave the asphalt road, turn down the alley, follow the mud path to the corner and go sharp right by the water pump.

There's a row of shanties here, immediately on the edge of the railway line, where the commuter trains trundle past several times an hour, deafening in their noise, spewing diesel filth into the heavy air.

This one-room shack is the home of nine-year-old Panchugopal Das and his family. His dad is ill with cancer and cannot work. His mum works long hours as a domestic.

Like so many other parents across the world, this couple's hopes rest on the shoulders of their children.

17-year-old Amman attends a government school and will soon sit his exams. He hopes to join the police force.

Young Panchugopal's prospects are even brighter. He is a pupil at Calcutta Emmanuel School, one of the best English-medium schools in the city, and is sponsored by Global Care. The best jobs – in the civil service and government – go to those who can speak English, who attend the English-medium schools.

Panchugopal's father wept as he said: "I never dreamed that one of my sons could go to such a place. Thank you for giving our whole family hope."

```
More than 3 billion people - almost half the world - each live on less
than US$2.50 a day
```

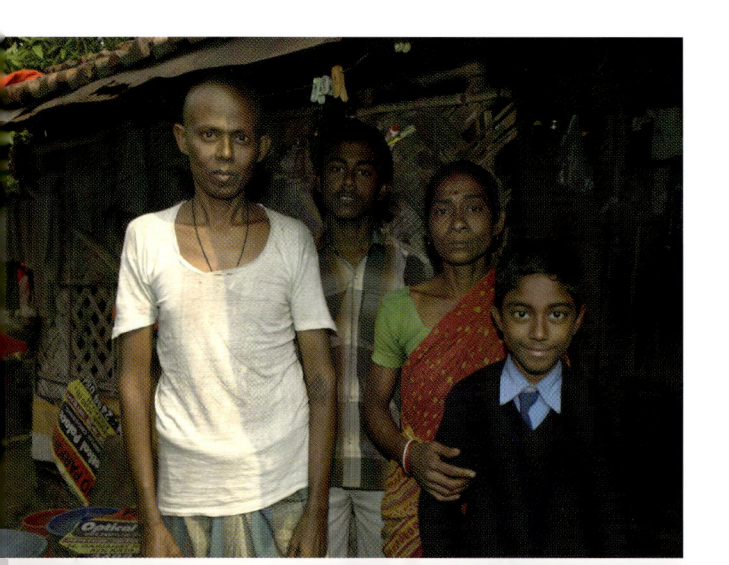

Listen to my prayer O God. Do not ignore my cry for help! Please listen and answer me, for I am overwhelmed by my troubles… Give your burdens to the Lord and He will take care of you.

Psalm 55:1,2 & 22

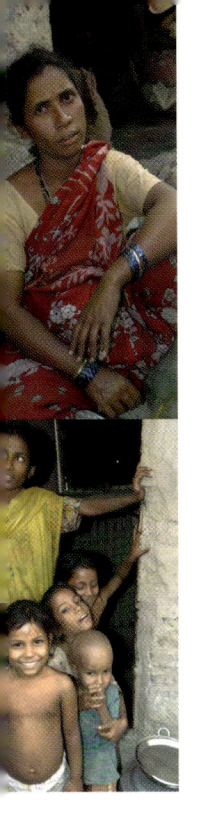

Fatima Bibi lives on the pavement in one of the worst slums of Calcutta. She was born on this street, she has brought up seven children on this street, and she will probably die on this street. It is the only home she has ever known.

Married at just 15, she is now 38, and pregnant with her eighth child. Her family lives in a one-room shelter made of bamboo and plastic sheeting, thrown up on the pavement.

Similar shanty dwellings line both sides of the alley. There is little room to move, almost no privacy, and no amenities – no toilets, no water, no electricity.

Fatima gets up at 2am every morning and begins the rounds of hotels and restaurants, sifting through used charcoal to scavenge coals fit for resale. She collects waste food too, to help feed her growing family, who typically eat just one meal a day. Her husband earns money singing religious songs, at mosques or other gatherings.

Together they earn about 30 rupees a day – enough to buy rice, or potatoes, oil and seasonal vegetables. It's not much for nine hungry people.

Yet Fatima hopes things will change for her children.

Her oldest son, Ashraf, now 16, spent five years studying at Global Care's Pavement Club and is now enrolled in a formal school.

Three of her younger daughters – Akbari, 8, Ansari, 7, and Anwari, 6, – are also enrolled at the Pavement Club. When little Akbar – just 3 – is old enough, he'll go too.

Learning basic numeracy, learning to read and write – Fatima knows these are skills which could change her family's lives forever.

THANK YOU

... for my electricity bill – my home has light and heat

...that the cash machine is out of order – I have money in the bank to provide for my family

... for feeling ill – I know I can visit a doctor

... for missing my train – because public transport is readily available

... when my washing machine breaks down – I wash my children's clothes with little effort

... when the kids are late home from school – education is free for every child in the UK

... when my tummy rumbles – I always provide good food for my children

... when my car breaks down – I am privileged to own a car

... when I've lost my specs – I am privileged to be able to see and have been taught to read and write

... when we run out of hot water – every day we have clean water on tap – no effort, no diseases!

No-one is a failure who has helped to hold happily a home together. Those who have been victorious in their homes can never be completely defeated.

Robert Burns

albania

Albania is one of the poorest countries in Europe. Global Care's work in the disadvantaged suburb of Bathore is recognised locally as a model of good practice, showing local people – and local authorities – that there is a way forward. It's innovative, effective, and it has a huge impact. But there is so much more we could do.

We discovered that under the face that is rough and nervous, and full of terrible experiences, still lives a child, although that baby never lived her childhood as she should. Her parents did not know how precious hugs are, what magic their kisses had to change the bad dreams into the most beautiful ones. So, they never gave kisses, what a miss…

Two months ago, a friend of the women's group committed suicide, she was only 27 years old and left three children. The 'child' inside this woman could not bear the violence for more than 27 years.

And the idea of suicide does not bother only one mind, almost all the women who are part of our group have thought of this act. They ironically laugh at the fact that they could not afford to buy the pills at the pharmacy.

But, what do we do? Six women, part of the Global Care Albania team, have trained as mentors. Mentoring, in Albanian culture, is really new as a concept.

The women could not understand how we could spend time with them alone, that the time we had was just for them. It is great to see them come and ask for an appointment and see that what they receive is just hope.

After the meeting, the situation was still the same, the economic and social conditions were not changed, but it is possible that in the midst of all the dark, they could see the light.

Every week we play together, laugh and share a topic. And after a meeting with these women they look so beautiful, so tender, so delicate and the child inside of them sometimes wakes up.

If only they could see her…

Evis Stafa, Global Care Albania

It is not a matter of thinking a great deal, but of loving a great deal, so do whatever arouses you most to love.
Teresa of Avila

She extends her hand to the poor. Yes, she reaches out her hand to the needy.

Proverbs 31: 20

In Bathore there have never been places for children to play. Eight years ago Global Care built a centre just for them.

It is one of the only places in Bathore where children come, are truly loved, respected, not violated and have the greatest fun. This is our biggest joy, seeing the children happy and bringing a smile to their faces.

It sounds like it is a centre only for children, but it is their centre even when they become teenagers, adults, mothers or fathers, and for their children again.

I did not know and I did not imagine the impact that an organization can have on one community.

I have seen many other organizations, yet when they left there was nothing left behind. For sure, what Global Care is doing here is totally the opposite.

In Bathore children don't celebrate birthdays. It is sad seeing a child saying 'today is my birthday' and not expecting any good wish, any rejoicing for the news and not expecting any present. It is supposed to be a joyful day for the family and the little one, but it is not. It is a normal rainy day, with the shoes leaking water inside as he walks to school, and the same dinner with beans and onion like every other day.

At Global Care Albania we decided to celebrate the birthdays of the ones who never celebrate: children, women and youth. It is very emotional creating a pleasing time for people who need it so much.

Evis Stafa, Global Care Albania

We ought not to grow tired of doing little things for the love of God, who regards not the greatness of the work, but the love with which it is performed.

Brother Lawrence

Sania was just 15 when her family arranged her engagement to a man twice her age.

She moved in with her husband's family, and her first task in married life was to boil some beans.

Sania put the beans in the pot, but not on the fire!

Not only was she totally uneducated, she had very few life skills. She truly didn't have a clue. When her mother heard about the beans she cried.

Sania is 40 now. She's learned a lot since then, but there are still a lot of issues no-one talks about. Since attending the women's group at Global Care's EJA centre, Sania's horizons have broadened beyond belief.

The information she receives, and the discussions with women of her own age and culture, offer an invaluable opportunity.

Ignorance really isn't bliss.

Sania's 16-year-old daughter will be starting her married life with more skills and knowledge than her mother ever had.

Teach your children to choose the right path and when they are older, they will remain on it.

Proverbs 22:6

THANK YOU

... for my electricity bill – my home has light and heat

...that the cash machine is out of order – I have money in the bank to provide for my family

... for feeling ill – I know I can visit a doctor

... for missing my train – because public transport is readily available

... when my washing machine breaks down – I wash my children's clothes with little effort

... when the kids are late home from school – education is free for every child in the UK

... when my tummy rumbles – I always provide good food for my children

... when my car breaks down – I am privileged to own a car

... when I've lost my specs – I am privileged to be able to see and have been taught to read and write

... when we run out of hot water – every day we have clean water on tap – no effort, no diseases!

... for this pile of ironing – my children have all the clothes they need

uk

Grandmother, mother-of-five, pensioner… activist, pillar of the community, pioneer…

Even though Gwen Daley is approaching 70, she has as much energy as women half her age.

And she is living proof that you don't have to travel to developing countries to make a difference to children in need.

She has devoted her life, not just to her own children, but to supporting children and young people in her adopted city of Coventry, here in the UK, where she has lived since coming from Jamaica to be married, in the early 1960s.

Right from the start she threw herself into helping young people, not just teaching Sunday School – although she was Youth Director at her church for many years – but reaching out to young people living on the edge, the marginalised and excluded, including setting up a ministry to young men in a local prison and young offenders institution.

Over the years, she teamed this passion with work as a JP, as chair of Coventry and Warwickshire Women's Business Development Agency, as treasurer of Black Mental Health, as a community worker, caterer and busy mum and wife!

She also got to know a small local charity – Global Care – and became a supporter and regular volunteer in one of their charity shops.

All of these things came together when Gwen pioneered a new group in Coventry, aiming to empower young black boys and improve their educational attainment – Black Boys Can!

"We could see that in these times African, African-Caribbean and mixed race children – especially boys – were under-achieving badly," says Gwen. "We decided we would go all out to help them succeed."

An initial meeting for parents from Coventry's black community saw 19 boys signed up for a fortnightly Saturday School, teaching maths, IT, English, Black History and a lot of sport.

Today Black Boys Can has helped hundreds of young people in Coventry and their families; improving self-esteem, empowering parents and raising educational achievement in a community which often feels marginalised and excluded.

The boys-only Saturday 'Excellence Academy' is still going strong, and there are now also after-school activities for boys and girls, as well as a two-week summer school which attracts hundreds of children from across the city.

Over the years Global Care has supported Black Boys Can with grants for sports equipment and summer school funding – because you can't ignore the fact that sometimes charity begins at home!

It is easier to build a boy than to mend a man.   Anon

When I born I black

When I grow up I black

When I go in sun I black

When I scared I black

When I die I still black

And you white fellow

When you grow up you white

When you go in sun you red

When you cold you blue

When you scared you yellow

When you sick you green

When you die you grey

And you calling me coloured?

Unknown. Nominated by UN as the best poem of 2009.

I could have no greater joy than to hear that my children live in the truth.

3 John 1:4

THANK YOU

... for my electricity bill – my home has light and heat

...that the cash machine is out of order – I have money in the bank to provide for my family

... for feeling ill – I know I can visit a doctor

... for missing my train – because public transport is readily available

... when my washing machine breaks down – I wash my children's clothes with little effort

... when the kids are late home from school – education is free for every child in the UK

... when my tummy rumbles – I always provide good food for my children

... when my car breaks down – I am privileged to own a car

... when I've lost my specs – I am privileged to be able to see and have been taught to read and write

... when we run out of hot water – every day we have clean water on tap – no effort, no diseases!

... for this pile of ironing – my children have all the clothes they need

... for my wrinkles and greying hair – I am privileged to reach three score years and ten, when millions of children die before they are five and the average age at death is 45 or less in too many countries

postscript

It is easy to despair, to think, 'what can I do?' And it is even easier then to turn away and get on with life.

But having had the privilege of visiting many of these projects, for me there is no possibility of simply turning away.

I am constantly reminded, whenever I eat a hearty meal, or turn on a tap – THEY'RE STILL THERE! They don't have running water, or electricity, or even a bed.

Christina Rossetti writes:

"I might show facts as plain as day;

But since your eyes are blind, you'd say,

'Where? What?' and turn away."

A mother's heart is a heart that continues to love, long after that child has 'flown the nest'. Let our hearts be softened towards those children who will never have the security we have been able to afford our children, or the care we received from our own parents, and let us make a difference somewhere to someone.

I can't do everything, but I mustn't do nothing.

Make me an instrument of your peace.

Where there is hatred, let me sow love;

Where there is injury, pardon;

Where there is doubt, faith;

Where there is despair, hope;

Where there is darkness, light;

Where there is sadness, joy.

O Divine Master grant that I may not so much seek to be consoled as to console,

to be understood as to understand;

to be loved as to love.

For it is in giving that we receive;

It is in pardoning that we are pardoned;

And it is in dying that we are born to Eternal Life.